KEN VENTURI'S STROKE SAVERS

Books by Ken Venturi

KEN VENTURI'S STROKE SAVERS • 1986
(with Don Wade)

THE VENTURI SYSTEM • 1983
(with Al Barkow)

THE VENTURI ANALYSIS • 1981
(with Al Barkow)

KEN VENTURI'S STROKE SAVERS

As Seen on CBS

By Ken Venturi
with Don Wade

Foreword
by Pat Summerall

Atheneum   New York
1989

All the photographs in this book were specially taken
by Stephen Szurlej at the Eagle Creek Country Club
in Naples, Florida.

Atheneum
Macmillan Publishing Company
866 Third Avenue, New York, N.Y. 10022
Collier Macmillan Canada, Inc.

Library of Congress Cataloging-in-Publication Data
Venturi, Ken
  [Stroke savers]
  Ken Venturi's stroke savers: as seen on CBS / by Ken Venturi with
Don Wade; foreword by Pat Summerall.
    p.   cm.
  ISBN 0-689-70814-9
  1. Golf.   I. Wade, Don.   II. Title.   III. Title: Stroke Savers.
  [GV965.V44 1989]   88-32632   CIP
  796.352'3—dc19

Macmillan books are available at special discounts for bulk purchases for sales
promotions, premiums, fund-raising, or educational use. For details, contact:

Special Sales Director
Macmillan Publishing Company
866 Third Avenue
New York, N.Y. 10022

10 9 8 7 6 5 4 3 2 1

Printed in the United States of America

For the guys at CBS who make these tips possible,
because without them this book would not have been possible.

Contents

9 Foreword
11 Authors' Note

PART I: FUNDAMENTALS
14 The Correct Address Position – 1
16 The Correct Address Position – 2
17 Your Memory Isn't Good Enough
18 Anti-hook Medicine
19 Use Your Head
20 Two Keys to a Good Grip
21 Understanding Tension
22 A Rule of Thumb
23 Try a New Grip to Find Your Old Grip
24 Toes Out for a Better Turn
25 Keep Moving
26 A Tip on Tempo
27 Olin's Takeaway Tip
28 Learning to Love Long Irons
29 Two Lessons from Adversity
30 Draw a Stripe for Proper Teeing Height
31 Make Sure You Really Do Address the Ball

PART II: EQUIPMENT
34 Club Lies
36 Some Thoughts on Balls
37 The Correct Grip Size
38 Offsetting a Fade or Slice

39 Finding a Good Sand-wedge
40 Put Score Ahead of Pride
41 Driver vs. Two-wood
42 Follow the Dot

43 **PART III: ON AND AROUND THE GREENS**
44 Take the Spin Out of Those "Pressure" Chip Shots
46 Forget Your Favorite Club
47 Putt with a Wedge from the Collar
48 Putter from the Rough
50 Targeting Your Sand Shots
51 The Texas Wedge
52 Controlling Your Sand Shots
54 Clip It off the Tee
55 Chipping from Sand
56 Playing from Wet Sand
58 The Blind Pitch Shot
59 Grass Bunkers
60 The "No-cut" Cut Shot
62 Plugged in the Upslope
64 Ball Way Below Your Feet
66 Ball Way Above Your Feet
67 Up the Bank
68 Too Much Reading Can Hurt
69 Reading Grain
70 Watch the Entire Putt

71	Putting Imagery	95	Hogan's Thoroughness
72	Targeting Breaking Putts	96	The Arm Shot
		98	The Deliberate Quick Hook
73	**PART IV: PLAYING THE GAME**	100	Fading the Ball
74	Some Thoughts on Learning	101	The Low Slice
75	Two Ways to Look at the Ball	102	The Downhill Lie
76	Warming Up	103	The Uphill Lie
77	Finding the Right Swing Thought	104	Playing from a Divot
78	Beating the Awkward-lookers	106	The Fairway Bunker Shot
79	Make All Your Shots Trouble Shots	108	The Backhander
80	Play at the Speed You Live	110	The Knock-down Shot
81	The Pressure Points	111	The Safe Shot from Hardpan
82	A Ben Hogan Tip	112	Developing Distance
83	The Importance of Sound	114	Skipping a Ball Across Water
84	When—and How—to Lay Up	116	The "Superpitch"
85	On Those Bad Days . . .		
86	Some Thoughts on Etiquette	117	**PART VI: PRACTICE**
		118	Some Thoughts on Practice
87	**PART V: SHOTMAKING**	120	The Basics of Good Balance
89	Beating the Wind	122	The Divider Club
90	The High, Soft Pitch	123	Know Your Distances
92	Ball in Water	124	The Four-tee Drill
93	Crosswinds	125	A Tip on Long Putts
94	The Flop Shot	126	One Last Thought
95	Taming the Hills		

Foreword

First of all, we are contemporaries. Same age, same sign — both Taurus — both gray (prematurely, I might add), and both love the same things about life. And, luckily, both of us athletically enjoyed some time in the limelight — he more than me.

I knew Ken, met him, during his active golfing career, but that was to know the name and the reputation. It was not to know "Ventura," as we call him.

I can still recall, vividly, the pictures in the Washington *Post* and other papers across the country of his great and trying victory at Congressional when he won the U.S. Open in 1964. I admired his courage and his courtesy. But all that was before I knew and worked with Ken Venturi — the friend and the man.

We have been together now for some eighteen years, much of it sitting side by side, looking at each other eyeball to eyeball. When you work as we have worked, you come to know a man heart to heart, soul to soul, and love to love. I've seen Kenny come to the tower with every emotion. With a broken heart. With anger. Hurting physically and deeply concerned about uncontrollable things in his life — a life filled with uncertainties.

I've also seen him come to the tower when everything is "plus" — rolling high, full of happiness and full of mischief.

But, no matter the mood, when Ken Venturi comes to work, he's ready. If it's one of his now-famous golf tips, he has every facet totally at his command, and it always amazes me how many he does in one take. And, by the way, although the tips are done early in the day, they always attract a lot of people, and he spends hours with the galleries. He loves people.

On the tower, as we work as broadcasters, we become colleagues, partners, teammates, and friends. . .and I'm not sure of the order. All I know is that some time or another, we are all going to need help. If Ken can help me, he will; and if I can help him, I will.

He does countless charity works. He deeply loves his family. He's a devoted and dear friend. I am most thankful to know him and sit beside him.

Now, if only one day he'll take me to another lunch at Scomas in San Francisco. . . .

PAT SUMMERALL

Authors' Note

When the CBS Stroke Savers began four years ago, the idea behind them was simple: Give the viewers quick, common-sense tips to help them improve their games and, by extension, have more fun practicing and playing. No great cosmic theories. Just clear, concise ideas that offered golfers a fighting chance at lower scores.

Nothing much has changed. When we began work on this book, the basic concept was the same. The idea was to take the tips that had previously aired and turn them into a book. Then, as we talked, one tip led to stories and ideas that, in turn, evolved into one, two, even three new tips. As a result, quite a few of the tips in this book have not yet aired.

Reading through the book is like going to a tour event and observing the players. Pay close enough attention, and you can learn the fundamentals that turn good golfers into very good ones—and the subtleties that turn the very good into the great. Some of the tips have to do with shot making and some with practicing. There's advice here on equipment, strategy, the full swing, the short game, and trouble shots from all over. We even threw in a few thoughts on etiquette.

In short, we've tried to cover golf's waterfront with this book, providing instruction that's easy to understand and to incorporate into your game. To the extent that our Stroke Savers become your stroke savers, this book has been successful.

KEN VENTURI
DON WADE

11

PART 1

FUNDAMENTALS

THE CORRECT ADDRESS POSITION –1

After a bad grip, the most common fault I see among golfers is an incorrect address position. Think about it for a second. If you start out in a bad position, what are your chances of making a good swing?

The three main faults I see are weight on the toes, knees locked, and bending from the waist instead of flexing the knees.

One reason for these faults is that people instinctively position the ball too far away from their bodies because they think this will give them a more powerful swing. Of course, that's

INCORRECT

14

wrong. As Byron Nelson once said, it's almost impossible to stand too close to the ball.

In the photographs you see examples of the correct and incorrect positions. Compare your address position with the photos, and if you look more wrong than right, try the following.

Flex your knees about as much as you would if you were going to dive into a pool. Set your weight back more toward your heels. Drop your head, look at the ball, and set the club behind it by letting your arms hang loosely. There, now that's the correct address position for you.

CORRECT

THE CORRECT ADDRESS POSITION—2

I've often heard "... and then he worked himself into position to hit the ball." I think most players work themselves *out* of position. For most, the first position taken is the correct one. The problem is that people address the ball, look back at the target, adjust their feet, look back at the target, move their feet again... and by now have managed to work themselves totally out of position.

Try to develop a routine that allows you to set up to the ball, look at the target once—twice at most—then pull the trigger.

YOUR MEMORY
ISN'T GOOD ENOUGH

Golf is a game of finding what works, losing it, and finding it again. Here are two tips that will help you find the swing that works best for you after it's been missing for a while.

Like most good players, I often place clubs on the ground when practicing to check that I'm properly aligned to my target and that my ball position is correct. One day while doing this, I noticed that, when I was in my correct driver address position, my left toe would point to the base of my 8-iron grip and my right toe would point to the hosel. If I set the clubhead of my 7-iron behind my left heel and ran the club straight out to the ball, it would give me the proper ball position—just opposite my left heel. I could then run a 5-iron parallel to the target line to make sure I was lined up squarely to the target.

These clubs happen to work perfectly for me. Depending on your height and stance width, you may need to use different clubs. But by using this drill when you are hitting the ball well, you'll be able to find your correct address position on those days when it seems lost.

A similar tip is to take three tees and mark the position of your toes and the ball when you are making good swings. Once you've marked them, measure the distance between your toes and from your left toe out to the ball. Record the measurements and refer back to them when you find yourself getting out of position at address.

ANTI-HOOK MEDICINE

If you have to fight a hook, it may be that you are setting your hands ahead of the ball at address or sliding them ahead of the ball as part of your forward press. If that's the case — and you have a good lateral move on the downswing, as most good players do — you are putting yourself in a position where the left hand can't help but release, or turn over, at impact. This results in a hook as the right hand turns on the power, causing the toe of the club to close or turn in as it meets the ball.

By setting your hands *behind* the ball at address, as Ben Hogan did, you put the left hand in a stronger position to resist the force of the right hand. Thus the key to fighting a hook isn't weakening the right hand, but strengthening the left.

USE YOUR HEAD

One subtle but interesting difference between good players and higher handicappers is the way they look at the target once they address the ball.

The good player will *rotate* his head to look at the target, whether it's the fairway, the green, or the hole.

"Working your head under" in this manner isn't a natural movement, which is why most players lift up their heads in checking on their target. This lifting and lowering of the head is an unnecessary motion and one that can cause you to "come over the top" on your downswing, creating either a slice or a pulled shot by throwing the clubhead outside the proper inside-to-down-the-line swing path.

CORRECT

TWO KEYS TO A GOOD GRIP

A proper golf grip is an unnatural act. Put a baseball in a person's hand for the first time, and he'll instinctively grip it and throw it properly. Do the same thing with a golf club, and he will grip it improperly and uselessly.

Here are two tips that will help you find a good grip.

First, the club should rest comfortably in the fingers and palm of the left hand. Second, stick your right hand out as though you were holding an imaginary pistol, then apply the right hand — in that position — to the club so that the thumb of the left hand fits comfortably along the lifeline which runs between the pads of your right hand.

Now you have a grip that will work for you — if you will spend the time to practice it until it becomes comfortable.

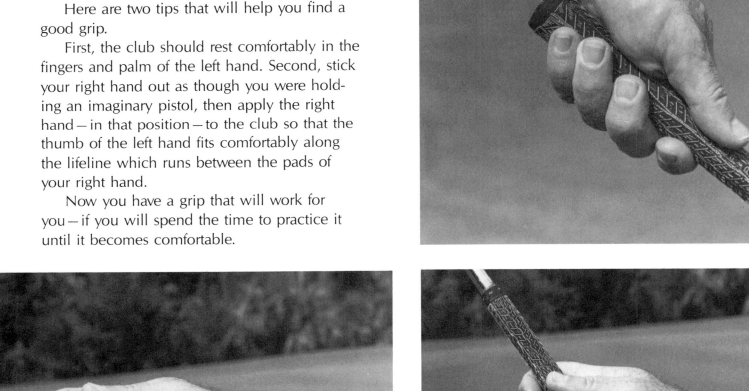

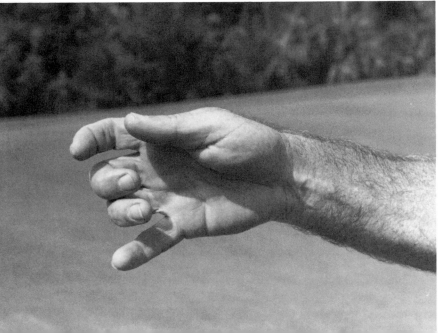

UNDERSTANDING TENSION

I've always felt that excessive tension in the golf swing begins with the grip. People who put a "death grip" on the club will find that their muscles tighten right up their forearms and into their upper arms and then across the chest. With that much tension it's impossible to make any kind of a smooth, consistent golf swing.

I've heard people say that you should grip the club the same way you would hold an egg or a bird—firm enough to keep control but not firm enough to do any damage. I prefer a comparison with fencing. A fencer must be able to hold his foil tight enough to have control, but lightly enough to allow his hand to move quickly and accurately.

A good way to insure against too much tension in your swing is to test your Tension Area. Grip the club and address the ball. It's natural to have a little tension in your forearms, but if there's so much that it has spread into your upper arms and chest, relax your grip slightly. I think you'll like the results.

A RULE OF THUMB

Your left thumb can help you regulate the length of your swing. To shorten your swing, draw the thumb up the grip. To lengthen your swing, run the thumb farther down the shaft.

You must still make a good body turn, but this rule of thumb will take care of the rest. Try it. You'll be amazed by the difference.

SHORT THUMB FOR SHORTER SWING

LONG THUMB FOR LONGER SWING

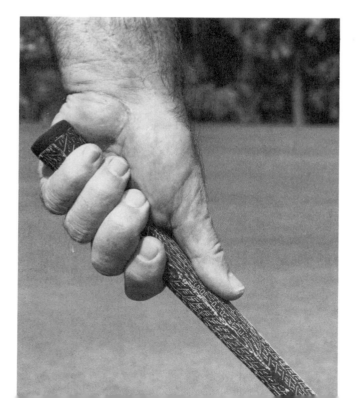

TRY A NEW GRIP
TO FIND YOUR OLD GRIP

I play with a Vardon or overlapping grip and always have, because it's the grip I'm comfortable with.

There are times, however, when I just can't get a good feel for the club. When that happens, I grip the club with an interlocking grip, where the forefinger of my left hand and the little finger of my right hand are intertwined. This is the grip used by Jack Nicklaus and Tom Kite, to name just two top players who favor it. The interlocking grip brings my hands closer together; then, once I've gripped the club, I simply move my little finger and assume my regular Vardon grip. This helps me to rediscover my proper grip feel . . . and I bet it will help you find yours too.

TOES OUT FOR A BETTER TURN

Many players, particularly as they get older and less limber, have a tough time making a proper turn, and as a result, they lose distance. One solution is to turn or toe-out your feet a little more, with the left foot toed-out slightly more than the right. Too often people confuse the term "square stance" with turning their toes in so their feet are at right angles to the target line. This toed-in stance restricts body movement.

So remember: Toes in restricts your turn, whereas toes out gives you the freedom to turn — and to turn on the power.

RESTRICTIVE

TURN-PROMOTING

KEEP MOVING

One thing that makes golf different from — and I think more difficult than — other sports is that it is one of the few sports where the player must initiate the hitting action. In most sports the player essentially reacts — to a pitch, to a serve, to the actions of another player, or whatever.

One way to overcome this cold-start factor is to keep moving at address. Waggle the club. Shift your weight. Move your feet slightly. Anything you can do, however slight, to keep moving will help when the time comes to pull the trigger and begin your swing.

For the player who keeps moving, the beginning of the swing isn't a static moment that begins with the hands or hips or whatever. For that player, the swing is just the continuation of a movement that flows through the entire act of addressing the ball.

A TIP ON TEMPO

It's difficult to exaggerate how important good tempo is to the golf swing. The old saying "Find me a guy with a fat wallet and a fast backswing, and I can be very happy" isn't far from the truth. A player can get by with some swing faults if he has good tempo.

One way to develop a good tempo for your swing is to watch—or think about—a player with outstanding tempo. Sam Snead is one player who always comes to my mind. I always found that my tempo was better when I played with Sam, and I bet yours will improve if you try to keep his swing—or his *kind* of swing—in mind when you practice and play.

OLIN'S TAKEAWAY TIP

Olin Dutra, the 1934 U.S. Open Champion, once showed me an excellent way to check if my move away from the ball — my takeaway — was putting me in good position for the rest of my swing. He told me to assume my address position, take my right hand off the club and extend it as you see here, then simply turn my upper body as if I were going to shake hands with someone approaching from the right.

Don't move your feet when you try this. Just make the turn with your hips and upper body. If you can duplicate that position when actually swinging the club, you'll be in good shape for the rest of the action.

LEARNING TO LOVE LONG IRONS

The long irons—the 1-, 2-, 3-, and 4-irons—are the most difficult clubs for the weekend player, because they have the least loft and, therefore, look intimidating and are less forgiving when mis-hit. As a general rule I advise higher handicappers to replace these clubs with fairway woods, which both look and play easier. However, if you want to stick with the long irons, the trick is to let the club do the work. Don't try to get the ball into the air by making a "scooping" swing, or try to *hit at* the ball instead of *swinging through* it.

Assume your address position, with the weight back toward your heels and the ball slightly left of center in your stance. Flex your knees, keep them flexed, and concentrate on making a long, smooth swing while driving firmly down and through the ball.

Sometimes it helps to imagine you have an 8- or 9-iron in your hands—a club you are comfortable with—and duplicate your swing with that club. Quite often, golf is a game of mind over matter.

TWO LESSONS FROM ADVERSITY

My friend Pat Browne is one of the best blind golfers in the country. In fact, he's a former champion of the United States Blind Golfers' Association. His courage, dedication, and love of the game would be lessons enough for all of us, but we can also learn from the way Pat and other blind golfers swing the golf club.

Pat's caddie describes the situation to Pat and then Pat visualizes the shot he wants to hit. That's lesson number one: Always visualize your shot. Since Pat can't see the ball, every swing is, in effect, a practice swing. This eliminates the impulse to hit *at* the ball. Pat swings the club smoothly from start to finish and simply lets the ball get in its way.

That's how we all should swing, and that's why our practice swings are our best swings: We don't think about the ball, only the flow and motion of the swing. And *that's* lesson number two.

DRAW A STRIPE
FOR PROPER TEEING HEIGHT

There seems to be a lot of confusion among middle-to-high-handicap golfers about just how high they should tee the ball when hitting a driver. Let's remove the confusion.

Take a felt-tip pen and draw a line around the middle of a ball. Then tee the ball so that the line, when set horizontally, is even with the top of your driver's face. This will put you in good position to sweep the ball off the tee.

If you still have a problem, you might try setting the ball at the proper height by using this method, then marking the tee with a stripe showing how far you had to stick it in the ground to achieve the proper teeing height. Once you've marked the tee, get a few others that are the same length and mark them at the same point. This way, all you have to do is sink the tee into the ground until the mark is flush with the turf, and the ball will be teed at the proper height.

MAKE SURE YOU REALLY
DO ADDRESS THE BALL

Many times golfers make the mistake of not adjusting their setup to the level of the ball when it is sitting up in the rough or settled down in a depression. As a result, unless they compensate during the swing, they'll mis-hit the shot.

My suggestion: When the ball is sitting up, align the sole of the club with the bottom of the ball. The best way to do this is to choke down on the grip. When the ball is down in a depression, increase your knee flex on the downswing a little to be sure of driving the clubface solidly into the back of the ball.

LIKELY TO PRODUCE A POP FLY OR A SHANK

SETUP FOR A SOLID HIT

31

PART II

EQUIPMENT

CLUB LIES

I've always enjoyed learning about equipment and working on my own clubs. Maybe that's one reason it surprises me that so many players — even good players — take so little interest in, or know so little about, their clubs. People don't realize that even something as relatively simple-sounding as the lie of a club — the way it rests on the ground — plays a big role in the kind of shots produced.

For example, when a club is too upright, the player will tend to hook or pull the ball, because the heel of the club catches the turf first, allowing the toe of the club to close too quickly. You will also tend to hit more fat shots if a club's lie is too upright for you.

On the other hand, if a club is too flat, you'll tend to hit the ball more off the toe of the club, producing more thin, pushed, or sliced shots because the toe of the club strikes the turf first, keeping the face open through impact.

Here are three quick ways to check the lies on your clubs.

1. The Divot Test. A shallow divot that is deeper on the outside than the inside is a sign that your clubs are too flat. A divot that is deeper on the inside (or heel side) indicates that your club is more upright than it should be to fit your swing.

2. The Business Card Test. Assume your normal address position with an iron and have a friend slide a business card under the sole of your club, beginning at the toe and sliding the

GOOD

BETTER

card toward the middle of the club. (This is best done on a hard surface.) If the card reaches the middle, and you can slide another card equidistant beginning at the heel of the club, then the lie is perfect. If you can slide the card just

PERFECT LIE

LIE TOO FLAT

from the toe to the middle of the club, that's still good, although not quite perfect.

3. The Lines Test. This test is a little more complicated, but it will tell you immediately if your clubs have the right lie for you.

Most irons have vertical scoring lines that run up the clubface. Take those notepad pages with the gummed edges and apply them to the vertical scoring lines so that the paper extends above the top line of the iron (see illustration). Now assume your normal address position. If the lie is correct, the lines—and the paper—will parallel the target line. If the lie is too flat, the lines will angle to the far side of the target line. If the lie is too upright, the lines will angle to the near side of the target line.

One other suggestion: Once you find the

LIE TOO UPRIGHT

lie that's best for you, take your set to your professional and have all the lies checked. Even though quality control is better now than when I started playing, very few manufacturers are perfect.

SOME THOUGHTS ON BALLS

I really believe most golfers would be better off playing a two-piece ball, if only because it's more durable and will better hold up to the punishment of missed shots.

However, if you are a good player, here are two points to remember. First, a balata-covered wound ball is easier to maneuver because it is easier to spin, both sideways and backwards, and will stop faster on the greens. Second, the higher-compression balata ball will stop even faster than a softer-compression ball. Why? The harder ball grips the scoring grooves on a clubface, while a softer ball absorbs the scoring action, resulting in less spin. In fact, if you really pinch a 100-compression balata ball, it will look like you ran a rasp across the cover—which is why, if you plan to play balata, it helps either to be rich or to have a friend in the ball business.

THE CORRECT GRIP SIZE

There is no one, standard, correct grip size for everyone. It all comes down to feel; some people will prefer a grip either slightly thicker or slightly thinner—and note my emphasis on *slightly*—than the standard size most manufacturers put on their sets.

With the club gripped in your left hand, if your fingertips just touch the pad of the thumb, then the grip is a pretty good fit for you. However, because altering grips is an easy and inexpensive job that pros can often do while you wait, it's worth experimenting. For most golfers, what feels best will also work best.

OFFSETTING
A FADE OR SLICE

The vast majority of weekend players hit the ball with either a slice or a fade, and for that reason I think they could do themselves a big favor by getting irons that are slightly offset. By offset, I mean that the bottom, or leading, edge of the club faces are set back slightly from the hosel (the part that connects head to shaft).

The best way to check if your irons are offset is to hold one like a rifle, with the butt end of the grip near your eye and the toe of the club pointing toward the ground. Sight down the shaft. If the iron is a traditional grind, you will see just a hairline of the leading edge. If it is offset, you won't be able to see any of the leading edge.

FINDING A GOOD SAND-WEDGE

I've always prefered a "weak" sand wedge—i.e., a club with at least 58 degrees of loft—because that's enough to virtually guarantee that I can get out of any bunker. I never wanted a sand club I could hit more than 60 or 70 yards. Pitching wedges are designed for those shots, and, with practice, you can learn to hit them high and land them softly.

I want a sand club to have a fairly wide flange, but not much bounce.* That's because, if I'm trying to fit a shot into a pin that's tucked tightly, I don't want the club bouncing and skidding all over the place at impact.

I'd rank a good sand club right up there with the driver and the putter in terms of tools in which you want to have maximum confidence. And if you are going to develop confidence in a club, you'd better spend a lot of time choosing just the right tone.

*"Bounce" is a combination of the width of the flange—the distance between the leading and trailing edges of the flange—and the difference in height between the leading and trailing edges.

PUT SCORE AHEAD OF PRIDE

If you just can't master the long irons, I suggest you swallow your pride and replace them with 5-, 6-, and 7-woods. They are more forgiving and less intimidating than long irons, and, in the final analysis, what matters are the numbers you post, not the clubs you made them with.

DRIVER VS. TWO-WOOD

It's no coincidence that a lot of people who have trouble hitting long irons also have a difficult time with drivers. Chiefly, that's because, when they set up to the ball, they are looking down at a club that doesn't have much loft and, as a result, either consciously or subconsciously try to "scoop" the ball into the air.

If you are such a player, you could save yourself a lot of trouble by either trying a driver with more loft than normal — say 11 or 12 degrees — or forgetting the driver altogether and putting a 2-wood in your bag. A 2-wood has 14 degrees of loft, and the smaller head also looks less intimidating. The added loft will help you get the ball airborne, as will the shallower clubface.

FOLLOW THE DOT

A while back I began to have some trouble with my putting. It was difficult for me to keep the putter moving on the proper line. To solve this problem, I put a spot of white paint out toward the toe of the putterhead. Now, my only concern is that the white dot moves on a straight line throughout the stroke.

It's a lot easier to focus on that dot than it is to focus on the entire blade.

PART III

ON AND AROUND
THE GREENS

TAKE THE SPIN OUT OF
THOSE PRESSURE CHIP SHOTS

The last thing I want to worry about when I have a tough chip shot is how much the ball is going to check up because of backspin. Unless it's a special situation, I don't want the ball to bite at all.

To take the spin out of a chip, you've got to take the wrists out of the shot. To do this, open your stance slightly, set the ball back—at least to the middle of your stance—and address the ball with your hands well ahead of the ball. Keep your hands ahead of the clubface until impact and make sure to hit the ball with a slightly descending blow.

By setting the ball back, you help ensure that the clubface will close down slightly at impact, causing the ball to roll smoothly toward the hole with little, if any, backspin. This technique is particularly important when you find yourself playing under pressure, because it allows your big arm and shoulder muscles to control the shot and helps eliminate the role of the smaller hand muscles—muscles that can get twitchy under pressure.

A good way to learn this shot is to slide a wooden tongue depressor or coffee stirrer under your glove or watchband so that it rests along the top of your left wrist and hand. This prevents your wrist from breaking down and helps ensure that you strike the ball with a descending blow.

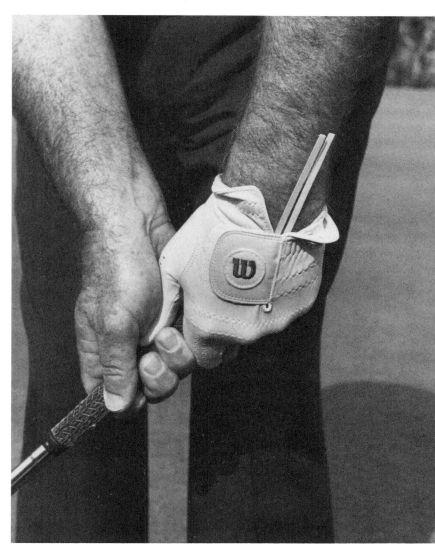

45

FORGET YOUR FAVORITE CLUB

If there is one mistake that most middle-to-high-handicappers make around the green, it's in trying to hit all their chip shots with their favorite club. This is a mistake, because, instead of changing clubs to suit the situation, you have to change your swing—obviously a needless complication in an already complex game.

Assuming you have a good lie, the clubbing decision should be based on how much fringe you have to carry and how much the ball needs to roll once it settles on the green. Since you want to spin the ball as little as possible, I suggest taking the least-lofted club possible, right on down to the 5-iron.

Spin is a variable that is difficult to judge and control—and control is the top priority on delicate shots like these.

PUTT WITH A WEDGE FROM THE COLLAR

You've hit a pretty good approach, but the ball rolls through the green and the fringe, and comes to rest against the first cut of rough that makes up the collar of the green.

You could try to use a putter, but the smarter shot is to putt with your sand wedge.

Assume your normal putting stance and grip, but choke down on the wedge so that the leading edge of the face is lined up with the equator of the ball. Also, take particular care to make sure that the leading edge is lined up dead square to the ball. Make your regular putting stroke, contacting the ball where it rises above the rough. The weight of the flange will give you a nice, solid contact and a good roll.

PUTTER FROM THE ROUGH

I thought I'd seen everything in golf, but a few years ago a friend showed me a shot that really impressed me.

When you're in the rough just off the green, it's often tough to catch the ball cleanly with a wedge, particularly if it has settled well down in the grass. If the ball is 60 feet or more from the hole, try playing it with a putter instead of a wedge.

Set up with a square stance, but position the ball *outside* your right foot. Hold the club with your putting grip and set your hands well ahead of the ball. Pick the club up steeply and drop it sharply on the ball. The ball will pop into the air, skip onto the green, and settle quickly into a smooth roll. This is a shot that takes practice, but it's also a shot that works—and it will definitely surprise your friends.

TARGETING
YOUR SAND SHOTS

Golfers often complain that they hit their sand shots to the right of the hole after they've opened the blade of the sand wedge for added loft. I tell them the problem is that they've put the cart before the horse.

Most golfers assume their stance aimed squarely to the target, *then* open the clubface. The correct method is first to set the blade open to the proper degree and aim it at the target, then to build your stance around the clubface, with your feet and shoulders set open and aimed left of the target. This allows you to slide the club under the ball, taking a long, shallow cut of sand and sending the ball directly toward the target.

THE TEXAS WEDGE

The Texas Wedge—using a putter from off the green—is one of the safest yet most misunderstood shots in golf.

The problem is that people tend to move the ball back in their stance and then pop down on it with a descending blow. That can cause two things to happen—both bad. One, the ball jumps into the air and bounces off line as it travels toward the hole. Two, the ball is driven down into the grass and loses speed, ending up well short of the hole.

To avoid both, play the ball forward in your putting stance—off the left heel—and widen your stance by moving the right foot back slightly. This gives you a firmer foundation for the stroke. Set your hands slightly behind the ball, which adds loft to your putter, and then make your normal putting stroke.

I think you'll be surprised at how smoothly the ball rolls toward the hole—and how many shots this will save you in the course of a round.

CONTROLLING
YOUR SAND SHOTS

Just getting the ball out of a bunker is so diffi-cult for most players that they often don't even try to control the distance the ball carries. If they do, the mistake they make is trying to control the shot by varying either the length of the backswing or the force of the swing.

I believe it's easier to control the length of a greenside sand shot by the length of the follow-through: shorter for short shots, longer for longer shots, while making the same length backswing at a consistent speed.

One other tip. A key to successful sand play is flexing your knees at address and *maintaining* that flex throughout the shot. Too often, people vary their knee flex during a sand shot, which affects how the clubhead strikes the sand, resulting in either a thin hit (producing a skulled shot) or a fat hit (which usually means the ball stays pretty much where it was).

SET KNEE FLEX AND MAINTAIN IT THROUGH SWING.

CLIP IT OFF THE TEE

The standard advice for hitting a sand shot is to "hit two inches behind the ball." That wouldn't be bad advice if all traps had the same type and firmness of sand. But, since they don't, here's a better way.

Think of the ball as if it were sitting on a tee buried in the sand; then, instead of worrying about how far behind the ball to hit, just try to clip the ball off the tee. It's a lot easier to remember and a lot easier shot to hit.

CHIPPING FROM SAND

In the 1964 U.S. Open, I came to the final hole with a four-shot lead. I was literally exhausted, drained by the pressure and the intense heat and humidity, and playing solely by instinct. The green was guarded by water on the left, so I hit the safe shot, blocking my approach to the right side, where it landed in a bunker—not the ideal place but certainly better than in the pond.

I do not remember hitting the explosion shot I played, but, later, when I saw a film of that hole, I broke into a cold sweat. I had played the wrong shot. True, it had worked, but I could easily have misplayed it, sent the ball across the green into the water, and cost myself the Open. The smart shot would have been to chip the ball with either a sand or pitching wedge. It would have been the smart shot for me that afternoon in 1964, and it is the smart shot for you today when the circumstances are right.

First, you must have a good lie in a bunker with little frontal lip, and, second, you must have plenty of green to work with because the ball will run. Play the ball back in your stance and set your hands well ahead of it, then make the stroke strictly with an arm swing. There should be very little movement of your body or legs, and avoid breaking your wrists as much as possible, controlling the shot instead with the big muscles of your arms and shoulders.

One more thing about that shot back in 1964: It still scares me when I think about it.

PLAYING FROM WET SAND

Wet sand is both heavier and more compacted than dry sand and, therefore, requires a different type of sand shot. You need to make a shorter and more forceful swing, but you must also guard against losing control.

Square the face of your sand club to the ball so that it will cut cleanly into and through the sand. Widen your stance slightly for better balance and square it up. Flex your knees and keep them flexed the same amount throughout the shot.

Make a shorter, flatter backswing, driving the clubhead into the sand behind the ball and allowing the sand to throw the ball onto the green. The ball will come out faster and roll farther than it will from dry sand, so allow for the additional roll.

One last point: On any shot of more than 40 yards, I'd recommend using a pitching wedge rather than a sand wedge. The mechanics of the shot remain the same, but the reduced loft on the pitching club makes it easier to hit the longer shots without overswinging.

THE BLIND PITCH SHOT

Golf becomes even more difficult when you can't see your target, which increases elements of confusion and doubt. This is especially true for delicate shots like short pitches, where you have a very small margin for error. Let's say you've missed an elevated green and can't see the hole, but know it's tucked close to the near edge of the green. All you can see is the top of the flag, and you know that, in order to get it close to the hole, you must just clear the edge of the rough. How do you play the shot?

First, forget the rough, because dwelling on a negative is just asking for trouble. Instead, think of the flagstick and visualize dropping the ball right on top of it.

Hold the club at the end of the grip, and take a stance slightly wider than normal, with your hands set ahead of the ball. Swing the club away with an early wrist cock, then let the clubhead drop just behind the ball at a sharply descending angle. The result will be a nice, soft lob shot.

One warning, though: Make sure you don't decelerate the club at impact because you are in a hurry to look up and see the results. Be patient, so that when you do look up you'll like what you see.

GRASS BUNKERS

If you golf around the country, you'll notice that more and more new courses have grass bunkers. They've been a part of the game since its beginnings in Scotland, but they are undergoing a resurgence here in the States now, and in that respect they may pose a new challenge for you.

Grass bunkers require a special type of shot if you find yourself in them around the greens. Because this isn't a shot where you need to work your legs, widen your stance and flex your knees. Grip the club very lightly, pick the clubhead up very abruptly and steeply on the backswing, then feel as though you're simply dropping the clubhead down on the ball. There's not much follow-through on this shot, but the steep angle of descent will get the ball into the air quickly and allow it to land softly.

Normally, you would play this shot with the ball positioned opposite your left instep, but, to hit it even higher and softer, experiment with playing it even farther forward in your stance.

THE "NO-CUT" CUT SHOT

When facing a delicate shot over a bunker to a tight pin placement, many players—especially good ones—open their stance and the clubface, then try to "cut" the ball in by sliding the clubface under it. This shot creates a lot of spin and, when done properly, is very effective. The problem is that the shot requires strong nerves, excellent timing, a lot of practice, and an awfully good lie. If you want a safer shot, try one I learned from an old friend.

Assume your normal address position, then weaken your grip by turning *both* hands to the left. This has the effect of leaving the clubface open at impact, but at the same time it allows you to make a firm, accelerating swing with your sand wedge.

The key to the shot is the acceleration, because, all too often, players decelerate through impact while trying to cut the ball softly. Frequently the ball then winds up in the bunker.

This "no-cut" cut shot isn't one that will travel very far forward, but it will pop up into the air nicely and land softly with a consistent roll.

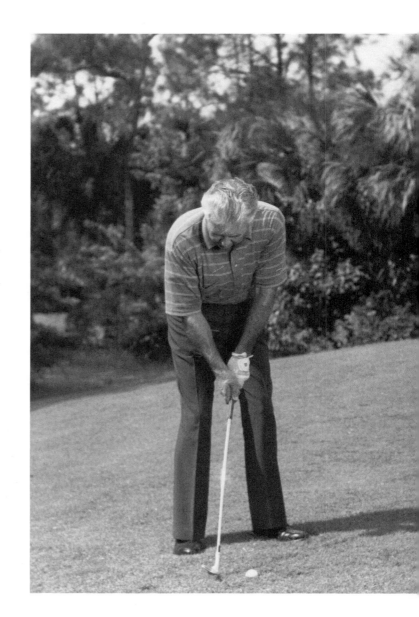

PLUGGED IN THE UPSLOPE

When you are playing a course with steep-faced bunkers protecting the greens, you'll occasionally plug an approach shot in a severe upslope, forcing you to address the ball with one foot outside the bunker. This is not an easy shot, but it *is* playable as long as you don't panic.

Plant your back foot solidly, because you want to guard against moving your body excessively on the shot. Set your hands ahead of the ball, then — and this is the key — adjust your shoulders so that they are parallel to the slope of the bunker. Pick the clubhead up sharply and drive it hard into the slope directly under the ball. There isn't any follow-through, and you must be firm with the swing.

In such cases you should never be thinking "close," but you should be able to get the ball out and on the putting surface every time.

BALL WAY BELOW YOUR FEET

This is a very tough shot, and the big temptation is to bend over from the waist in an effort to get fully down to the ball. I have a better idea. Widen your stance, hold your sand club at the very end of the grip, then *flex your knees* until the club is in position to hit the ball. The most important thing after that is to stay in your flex—keep your leg angles as they were at address. It's not a pretty shot, but it does work.

Incidentally, a number of good players have a slightly longer shaft put in their sand clubs just for shots like this. An extra inch or so can make a big difference in awkward shots around the green, and you can always comfortably grip down for normal shots.

GET DOWN TO BALL BY FLEXING KNEES, NOT BENDING FROM WAIST.

MAINTAIN KNEE-FLEX THROUGHOUT SWING.

BALL WAY ABOVE YOUR FEET

My friend Joe Spoonster, from Akron, Ohio, does a lot of work with golfers who are blind. One of the devices he developed is pictured here. It's a stick with a magnet on one end and a whiffle golf ball on the other. Joe developed it to help his pupils understand the relationship between the clubface and the direction the ball flies.

When I saw Joe's invention, it was like a light going on in my head. For years I'd known a ball above the feet would fly left and one below the feet would go right. As you can see from the photograph, Joe's device shows why the ball flies the direction it does when the clubhead is soled parallel to the sloping ground.

With that in mind, the key to the common shot you see here is to aim to the right of your target. Resist the temptation to play the ball forward in your stance, since that will make you pull the ball even farther left. Play the ball back in your stance and set your hands ahead of it, then swing your arms without letting your wrists break.

One other tip for this shot: Play it with an 8-iron rather than a higher-loft club.

UP THE BANK

This is a much easier shot than one played off a downhill lie, but that's no reason to take anything for granted.

Set your weight on your left foot, with your hands ahead of the ball, then lower your right shoulder to conform to the slope.

The real key is using a less-lofted club than you ordinarily would. You need it because the slope actually adds loft to the club. By using a wedge you run a good risk of popping the ball up higher than you want. I suggest a 7-, 8-, or 9-iron, depending on the distance to the hole. When you strike the ball, try to avoid driving the clubhead into the hill. Instead, shape your swing to follow the angle of the slope as much as possible.

TOO MUCH READING CAN HURT

It is obviously important to figure out a breaking putt, but too much reading can create more confusion than it resolves. For instance, if you study a putt from behind the ball and then from behind the hole, you run the risk of sending your brain mixed signals.

My rule has always been to study putts from behind the ball to judge the break, and then from the low side of the hole — the side the ball will break toward — to see how much the putt is either uphill or downhill. I figure that's just about as much information as my brain can handle at one time.

READING GRAIN

People often miss putts because they fail to take into account the amount the grain of the green will cause the ball to break. This is particularly true on Bermuda grass greens. Here are two tips that will help.

First, if you are reading the putt from behind the ball and the grass appears to be shiny, the grain is growing *away* from you, thus the putt will be faster than it might first appear. If the grass appears dull, the grain is growing *toward* you, and the putt will be slower.

A second way of judging the grain is to look at the grass around the hole. If the grain is growing north to south, for example, the north side of the cup will appear ragged or thin. That's because the roots of the blades are sheared off in cutting the hole. The blades on the other side aren't affected because only the tips are cut off.

WATCH THE ENTIRE PUTT

Too often golfers will sail putts well past the hole, then compound the mistake by not watching the ball until it stops rolling. That's like shooting yourself in the foot twice.

You should watch every putt carefully until the ball stops rolling, because that way you can learn how the putt will break coming back. The game is hard enough already without making it harder by missing out on information like this.

PUTTING IMAGERY

Here's a tip that will help you develop a better feel for the proper speed on both uphill and downhill putts.

With an uphill putt, imagine that you are actually putting to an imaginary hole *just beyond* the cup. When you have a downhill putt, strike the ball as if you were trying to get it to die at the lip of an imaginary hole cut *just in front* of the cup.

TARGETING BREAKING PUTTS

I'll watch a fellow line up a long, breaking putt, then set up to the ball and get ready to give it a roll. Just before he strikes the ball, I'll tell you whether he'll make a good putt. It's one of the safest bets I can make, and I don't even have to see where he's aimed. All I have to do is watch his eyes.

Usually a player reads the putt, chooses the line, and picks an intermediate target where he wants to start the putt. Now he's ready to go, but, at the last second, he steals a glance at the hole. Bingo! He's just sent a scrambled signal to his brain. He wants to roll the ball at one target, but now his brain is focusing on another.

The lesson is this: Once you've judged the speed of the putt and the line, focus on one target and have the confidence to go at it.

PART IV

PLAYING THE GAME

SOME THOUGHTS ON LEARNING

I've been very blessed to have played with — and learned from — two great masters of this game: Byron Nelson and Ben Hogan. In 1952 I did an exhibition tour in California with Byron, traveling with him for two weeks around the state by car. After each match he'd review my round, asking me why I played particular shots, telling me when I'd made the smart play and when I'd made a mental error. Later, when I went on tour, I had a chance to play with Ben Hogan. He was just the opposite. He never told me much unless I asked, but I learned by observing.

In a sense, I was taught by Michelangelo and I painted with Leonardo. The lesson I learned was that there are at least two ways to learn if you are willing to work hard — by listening and by observing. And they are both constant and never-ending processes.

TWO WAYS
TO LOOK AT THE BALL

Golf is a game of inches. In fact, sometimes it's a game of fractions of inches. That's why you want to give yourself every available edge. Properly positioning the ball for a putt or a tee shot can give you that little edge.

Golf-ball covers are molded in a way that leaves a seam running around the equator of the ball. Manufacturers will often stamp a trademark or other designation on the seam, while the name of the ball is in the center — at the poles — of each hemisphere.

When you drive the ball, you want to make contact on the poles, where the ball's name is stamped. This allows the ball to compress more easily than it would if you made contact along the seam.

However, when you putt, you want to roll the ball along the relatively dimple-free seam for a truer roll. You can also use the trademark stamped along the seam to help align your putts better. After you've lined up a putt, set the ball down so the trademark is pointed toward your target, then try to get the ball rolling in a straight line. If you push or pull the putt, you'll be able to tell by the way the trademark wobbles off line.

So, remember, hit it on the poles for power and on the seam for straightness.

WARMING UP

Golf must be the only sport where people show up to play without warming up, then can't understand why it takes them so long to get in the game.

Take a lesson from the pros. Allow yourself plenty of time to warm up. Develop a ritual around which clubs you hit to warm up and in what order. If you can't do that, at least swing a weighted club — or buy a weighted ring you can slip over the shaft to make a weighted club.

You've got to give yourself a fighting chance before you can win the fight to lower your handicap.

FINDING
THE RIGHT SWING THOUGHT

I can't overstress the value of warming up before a round. It loosens your muscles and helps get you mentally prepared to play. Warming up can have another benefit, too — it can give you a swing thought to keep in mind during the round. Swing thoughts are keys you can focus on to keep yourself in the groove.

Cary Middlecoff used to say that he had lots of swing thoughts that worked for him — the key was finding the ones that worked for him each particular day. And the place he looked for them was on the practice tee before his round.

Incidentally, someone once asked Bob Jones what his favorite swing thought was. "Whatever worked best last," Jones replied.

BEATING THE
AWKWARD LOOKERS

If you're like me, there are some holes you will never like because they just don't look right to you. The way these holes set up makes it difficult for you to visualize the shot you need to hit.

The ninth at Augusta National has always been like that for me, because it is a dogleg left but the terrain slopes to the right, creating an awkward approach shot to a very demanding green.

However, on this hole and others like it, I found that if I tried to "work" the ball—to either draw or fade the shot—it forced me to concentrate just that much harder, which helped take my mind off the awkwardness of the hole itself.

MAKE ALL YOUR SHOTS
TROUBLE SHOTS

Some golfers are surprised when they hit a good shot out of trouble. They shouldn't be. The truth is that, when you face a difficult shot, you usually concentrate better, think harder about what you have to do, and therefore generally pull the shot off. Another reason is that you focus more sharply on where you *have* to hit the ball.

Just think how much better you would score if you could focus that hard on all your shots.

PLAY AT THE SPEED YOU LIVE

The most successful golfers swing and play at the same speed they live. Take Tom Watson, for example. Tom has a fairly quick swing and plays at a brisk pace, and he's the same way off the golf course. Don January is just the opposite. He doesn't have a quick move in his game, and if he tried to play at Watson's speed, he might not break 80.

It's like driving a car. Some people are content at 35 miles an hour, while others aren't happy until they are pushing the speed limit. The trick is finding the cruising speed for your game that you feel comfortable with.

THE PRESSURE POINTS

When faced with a shot under pressure, it's only natural to become anxious, rush the swing, and rise up out of the shot to see where the ball is headed. Therefore, when I'm in a situation like this, I focus on maintaining my knee flex throughout the swing, which helps me more than anything to stay down through the shot.

My other thought in these situations is to keep my head down until my right shoulder brushes under my chin. By that time the swing is complete, and the ball is well on its way to the target.

A BEN HOGAN TIP

I learned a valuable lesson from Ben Hogan about playing under pressure. He told me that, when he was tense but had to make a long, smooth swing, he'd grip the club as far up the shaft as he could—his little finger would be right at the very top of the grip. This forced him to make a long, steady swing for fear of losing control of the club.

Too often, when people are under pressure, they want to choke down on the grip for added control. That might work in baseball, but it won't help in golf.

THE IMPORTANCE OF SOUND

When I was a kid growing up in San Francisco, I found that, if I tried to hit a shot with a plane flying over, I seldom made solid contact. The change in sound was distracting, and it threw off my concentration and balance just enough to cause a poor shot. Later, when playing in tournaments, I found that noise didn't bother me as long as it was consistent. In a sense it was like being a tight-rope walker. The reason tightrope walkers need the sound of a snare drum during their acts is that it drowns out other sounds and gives them a consistent background noise.

Sound is also the reason why I hate to wear a stocking cap in cold weather. Pulling the cap down over my ears makes it difficult to hear the club's contact with the ball. The sound of impact is a key factor to me, and it might be for you, too. So, in cold weather, try rolling your cap up above your ears before each shot.

WHEN—AND HOW—TO LAY UP

In the final analysis, golf is a game of playing the odds. The question the good player asks himself before every shot is this: Are the rewards worth the risk? The good player lets the *situation* dictate the shot that will be played.

If you decide to lay up on a given hole, there are three factors to consider. The first is what position gives you the best approach to the pin for your next shot, relative to hazards—water, bunkers, severe slopes, rough around the green, etc.

The second factor is what position gives you the most green to work with. The more green you have to hit to, the greater your margin for error.

The final consideration is giving yourself a *full* shot into the green. Too often people think they have to get as close to the green as possible when laying up. I think that's a mistake, since this often leaves you with difficult and delicate half- or three-quarter wedge shots. I say, leave yourself a distance you can cover with a full shot, using the sand wedge or pitching wedge, and then make that full swing. It's easier to put spin on the ball with a full swing, not to mention releasing pressure on your nerves—and on your scores.

ON THOSE BAD DAYS . . .

Every golfer has a fault he falls back into repeatedly. The trick is learning what that fault is and then, obviously, how to correct it. That's one thing that makes the good player consistently successful. He can have his swing go bad during a round and still be able to turn an 80-plus into a near-par round.

The secret is having an escape valve—a swing simplified enough to let you keep the ball in play without trying anything fancy. The good player doesn't experiment or force changes during a round. He just gets the ball around the golf course as best he can—avoiding gambles and playing the highest-percentage shots—and then heads for the practice tee to solve the problem.

SOME THOUGHTS ON ETIQUETTE

Golfers spend a lot of time and money taking lessons and trying to improve, but, without knowledge of the game's etiquette, they will never truly learn what golf is all about. Take something as simple as repairing ball marks. If you went to a Tour event and studied the final green after the last group of the day had finished play, I would defy you to find a ball mark. And the same goes for divots. Restoring the turf to playable condition is a matter of courtesy among good players.

Now, think about how many times you've played on greens scarred by unrepaired ball marks. Surprisingly, it's not always because people are lazy, but rather that they've never been taught the finer points of the game. Maybe all the new golfers ought to be required to take an etiquette test before being allowed on the course.

One major problem such a test might help correct is slow play. There's no excuse for a round that takes more than four hours, or for people tying up a course because they refuse to let faster groups play through when there is a hole open. All I know is that I'd rather play with an 85-shooter who plays fast than a scratch golfer who takes all day.

PART V

SHOTMAKING

BEATING THE WIND

When playing in a head wind, the biggest mistake golfers make is trying to hit the ball harder to keep from losing distance. All that does is put more spin on the ball and send it higher in the air, thus *losing* distance.

I say that if you are between clubs — say you are unsure whether to hit a 6-iron or 7-iron — take the 6-iron and concentrate on making a smooth, easy swing. You'll have better control, the ball will tend to fly lower because of the reduced loft of the club and the easier swing, and you'll have a better chance of cheating the wind.

THE HIGH, SOFT PITCH

One of the most important shots you can have in your bag is the high, soft pitch, for times when you must loft the ball over a bunker to a tight pin placement or face other situations that require a delicate shot.

Hold the club at the end of the grip. Address the ball with your knees comfortably flexed and your weight set back toward your heels. Set your hands ahead of the ball, which is positioned at the center or left center of your stance. Take the club away from the ball, with the clubhead, hands, and shoulders moving *in one piece*, to avoid quickly cocking your wrists.

The real secret of this shot lies in sliding the right knee to the left, toward the target, through impact. Also, always try to finish the swing with your hands nice and high.

BALL IN WATER

Most of the time when you hit a ball into water you're going to have to take a drop and accept the penalty. Still, there are times when conditions will permit you to play the shot and save a stroke.

As a general rule this is a very low-percentage shot unless at least some of the ball is above the water. Then, play the shot as you would from a buried lie in sand, using the sand wedge. Square the face at address, since this allows the club to cut through the water more easily. Knee flex is crucial to this shot, and it should actually increase through impact, because your legs act as shock absorbers.

Set your hands ahead of the ball, pick the club up sharply by setting your wrist cock early, then drive the clubhead sharply down into the ball, letting the water throw it out just as sand forces the ball out in a bunker. Forget about a follow-through.

If you are a pretty good player and the ball is totally submerged, you may still have a shot. I must stress, however, that it is an extremely risky shot that should be tried only if you absolutely *must* save a stroke — say, in the closing holes of a match or tournament.

Hitting a submerged ball is difficult for two reasons. First, the water distorts the image, making it appear that the ball is closer than it really is. Second, the flange on your club causes the clubhead to skip slightly when it initially strikes the water, much the same way a flat stone will skip on a pond. To compensate for these factors, think of the ball as sitting in a "fried-egg" lie in a bunker and play it the same way, aiming at a target three or so inches behind the ball.

Remember that it is a rules violation to ground your club in a hazard, so don't let the clubhead touch the water at address or on the takeway.

This isn't a shot you want to practice every day, but it is a fine excuse to invest in a good rain suit.

CROSSWINDS

I think it is a mistake for a good player to try to compensate for crosswinds by aiming wide of the landing area and allowing the ball to be blown back on target. The problem is that your brain takes over and subconsciously won't let you hit the ball as far off-target as you consciously plan to start it. The good player is better off aiming at the target and fading or drawing the ball into the wind to hold the shot on line.

The difference between a successful player and the others is that a successful player sees only the target — while everyone else sees only the trouble.

THE FLOP SHOT

Here's a good shot for getting close to tight pin placements, or for those situations when you need a high, soft shot over a bunker or greenside mound.

Play the ball off your left heel and take a fairly wide but comfortable stance. Flex your knees and maintain that flex throughout the shot — it's vitally important to resist any temptation to rise up out of this shot.

Beyond that, the key is making a long, soft, gentle swing — and the key to making that kind of swing is to grip the club at the very end of the shaft. Since it is a short shot, people often make the mistake of choking down on the shaft, which creates a shorter, quicker swing.

Play the flop shot with an open clubface, but experiment with the degree you open the blade. The more you lay open the blade, the higher and shorter the shot will fly.

TAMING THE HILLS

Hills make club selection more difficult, so here's a good rule of thumb. For every 25 feet that a green is elevated above you, take one club more.* For every 25 feet that the green is below you, take one club less.

HOGAN'S THOROUGHNESS

I played a lot of golf with Ben Hogan, and he never ceased to amaze me with how much he thought about every aspect of the game. People say nobody ever analyzed a course better than Ben, and I guess that's true. His attention to detail was legendary.

I remember one round when he pointed to a green and said to guard against hitting a shot to one side of it because that was where the players walked off. Hogan explained that the players would beat down the grass with their feet, causing the grain to run away from the green. That meant a pitch played from that area would be played against the grain, making the shot more difficult because the grass would tend to grab the club.

Now, *that* is attention to detail.

*In this section the terms "one club more" and "one club less" are frequently used. To clear up any confusion, an example of taking one club *more* would be hitting a 5-iron instead of a 6-iron. An example of hitting one club *less* would be hitting a 6-iron instead of a 5-iron.

THE ARM SHOT

When you get under pressure, the smart move is to play the safest, easiest shot you have in your bag. For me, it's what I call the arm shot.

Take one club more than you ordinarily would—a 6-iron instead of a 7-, for instance—because this isn't a shot you should be trying to muscle, but one you want to hit nice and easy. Take your normal address position, with the ball positioned just inside your left heel. Concentrate on keeping the clubhead low on the backswing, with little if any wrist cock. Then, coming down, drive firmly through the ball without breaking or releasing your wrists. In other words, you're making a shorter, more controlled swing, with a hold or abbreviated follow-through after impact.

As I say, this is a good shot to have under pressure, but it's also useful when the wind is behind you, because it helps get the ball in the air while still landing it softly.

The arm shot isn't played with a swing that allows you to fade or draw the ball, but it is a safe swing, and it is also a swing you can use to reduce the chances of hitting a flyer from the rough.

THE DELIBERATE QUICK HOOK

There will be times when you have to hit a low, hard hook, usually when you've driven the ball into trouble — say, into the woods on the left with a tree blocking your approach to the green. You have to "bend" the ball hard to get it curving back toward the green. This is the shot for that situation.

As a rule, I never alter my grip, but for this shot I'll take a "stronger" grip — that is, turn both hands slightly to the right on the club. This allows me to turn the toe of the club over quicker at impact, thereby producing the necessary right-to-left side spin on the ball.

TURN BOTH HANDS AWAY FROM TARGET TO STRENGTHEN GRIP.

I play the ball back in my stance, and close my stance by setting my feet, hips, and shoulders aimed to the right of the target. Most of my weight is on my left side. I *open* the clubface, address the ball off the heel of the club, and try to get a loose, flexible feeling in my hands and wrists. To hook the ball your hands have to be working very quickly at impact so that you can close the toe of the club through the ball ahead of the heel. Trying to finish the swing low and around your body will help accomplish this.

One last thing: If hit properly, the ball will come out low and hot, so allow for plenty of roll. There's not much point in hitting a great recovery, only to watch the ball roll into trouble behind the green.

CLOSE STANCE BY AIMING FEET, HIPS, SHOULDERS RIGHT OF TARGET.

FADING THE BALL

Over the years, good players develop—through practice and experimentation—certain keys to hitting certain shots.

When I want to fade the ball from left to right, I begin by opening my stance, so that my feet, hips, and shoulders are aimed to the left of the target. Next, I set my hands slightly ahead of the ball and grip the club a little tighter than normal with my left hand. This does two things. First, it keeps the clubface slightly open at the top of the swing. Second, and more important, it helps keep the left wrist from breaking down, or rotating, at impact, which, by keeping the clubface open through the ball, is the real key to fading shots.

OPEN STANCE BY AIMING FEET, HIPS, SHOULDERS LEFT OF TARGET

THE LOW SLICE

This is a good shot to have when you need to work the ball out of trouble. The first rule is to let the club do the work for you, by taking a less-lofted club than the distance requires. For example, a 5-iron will send the ball out lower than a higher-lofted club, so this eliminates trying to knock down or deloft a 7- or 8-iron. It's also easier to fade a less-lofted club, because the ball tends to cut across the blade more readily.

To hit the low slice, take the less-lofted club and open your stance so that your feet, hips, and shoulders are aimed left of your target. Swing the club away from the ball slightly outside the target line, since this will help keep your wrists from cocking too quickly. The key to this shot is to avoid breaking your wrists, keeping your hands working together as though they were in a cast. At impact, you want to drive through the ball, with the heel of the club leading the toe, thus keeping the blade open.

THE DOWNHILL LIE

Hitting from a downhill lie is particularly difficult because it is so easy to lose your balance. Your weight is set left at address, and then the motion of the swing moves you more to the left. That makes it very important to begin from a good, solid address position, with your left foot moved slightly more forward than normal, and your hands set ahead of the ball.

The common mistakes on this shot are catching the clubhead in the grass on the backswing and/or hitting the ball fat. The key to preventing them is aligning your shoulders *parallel to the plane of the slope,* which in this case sets your right shoulder higher than your left.

One other tip: You'll need to take one club less — 7-iron vs. 6-iron — for this shot, since the slope will tend to deloft the club, making it play stronger than it normally would.

BEGIN FROM A SOLID, STABLE SETUP.

SET SHOULDERS PARALLEL TO SLOPE.

THE UPHILL LIE

While it is not as difficult as a shot from a downhill lie, playing from an uphill lie still requires concentration and an understanding of the proper mechanics.

The common mistake golfers make is not taking the slope into account. As a result, they tend to drive the clubhead into the turf, hitting a "fat" shot.

The key to preventing this is aligning your shoulders to the angle of the slope, then shaping your swing to accommodate that angle. As you can see by the two clubs in the photograph, the angle of my shoulders is parallel to the angle of the slope. When hitting the shot, you want to feel that you are "sweeping" the ball off the grass rather than "punching" it away.

There are two other considerations to keep in mind when facing this shot. First, because the slope actually increases clubface loft, you should hit one club *more* — a 6-iron instead of a 7-iron, for instance. Second, the ball tends to fly right to left from an uphill lie, so allow for that curve when you aim at address.

ALIGN SHOULDERS PARALLEL TO SLOPE.

PLAYING FROM A DIVOT

The first thing you should do when you see that your ball has settled in a divot is tell yourself that it's a bad break, that it happens to everyone, and that you'll really have to concentrate on this shot. Working up a nice, hot anger about the whole thing isn't going to help one bit. Besides, the shot is not all that difficult.

Take one club more than you ordinarily would, widen your stance, and play the ball back toward your right foot, with your hands set well

NO

ahead of the ball. Flex your knees and maintain that flex throughout the shot. Pick the clubhead up sharply on the backswing, then drive down onto the ball with a steeply descending blow.

There's not much follow-through with this shot, the main thought being to make the most solid contact you can.

Oh, and you might also resolve never to leave a divot unrepaired yourself.

YES

105

THE FAIRWAY BUNKER SHOT

This shot scares most golfers—and the fact that it does makes it more difficult than it needs to be.

The first consideration is not how far you have to hit the ball to reach the green but your lie. If the ball isn't sitting up cleanly, you'll have to settle for taking a wedge and pitching the ball back into the fairway. This is no place to try to be a hero.

The second consideration is the height of the bunker's lip. The ultimate sin is trying to reach the green with an insufficiently lofted club and, instead, driving the ball up under the lip, because that's at least a two-shot mistake. Make sure you have enough club to get the ball *out* of the bunker with one swing.

Once you've selected the club, set up with the ball toward the middle of your stance, work your feet well into the sand, and set your hands ahead of the ball. You don't want a lot of movement with this swing. Control the swing with your shoulders and concentrate on hitting down on the ball first, and then into the sand. Think of this as almost a "half-topped" shot. Also, remember that, if you ground your club, it's a penalty.

If you are a good enough player to become comfortable with this shot, experiment by trying to "nip and hook" the ball. Set up as you would to draw the ball, then try to close the toe of the clubhead down over the ball through impact. This will give you added distance by creating more roll.

THE BACKHANDER

Has this ever happened to you? The ball comes to rest tight to the left side of a tree, rock, or other obstruction. You can't take your normal address position, and you can't putt the ball left handed, because it will get caught up in the rough. My solution is to turn your back on the problem.

Face away from the hole, taking a 7- or 8-iron, depending on the distance you have to carry. Choke down on the club, with the grip held firmly in the palm of your right hand. This is an arm swing. You *do not* hinge your wrist.

The key is to take plenty of practice swings so as to develop a feel for the shot, then concentrate very hard on the ball. Watch the ball intently enough, and you may just watch yourself save a penalty stroke for an unplayable lie.

THE KNOCK-DOWN SHOT

The wind is in your face, or it's gusting and swirling, making club selection difficult. What you need to do is hit a shot that takes the wind out of the picture. That shot is the knock-down shot. It's not difficult to hit, and it can save you a lot of headaches.

Take one club more than you think you need — say a 5-iron rather than a 6-iron. Choke down on the grip. Flex your knees and keep them flexed. Swing the club back low and slow away from the ball, and try to take it back straight away from the ball — neither inside nor outside the target line. This shot doesn't require a long, full swing — in fact, a three-quarter swing will usually do the job better. Drive the clubhead down and through the ball with a descending, punching blow while keeping your wrists — and especially your left wrist — firm.

There isn't much follow-through, because you really are just trying to punch the shot. The ball will stay low, but it will run. Most importantly, it will stay down below the wind.

THE SAFE SHOT
FROM HARDPAN

When playing from hardpan, it's difficult to make solid contact, because the club tends to bounce up off the hard surface before the leading edge can get fully under the ball. One way to protect against this is to take your wrists out of the shot by playing it almost as a long putt.

Begin by taking a wider-than-normal stance, because that will help keep your lower body motionless. Set your hands ahead of the ball and position the ball back toward your right foot. Now swing the club back *without* cocking your wrists, using just your arms and shoulders, then punch down on the ball.

You vary the distance the ball carries by your club selection. If you use a sand wedge, it's important that you set your hands well ahead of the ball to negate the bounce that is built into the flange. A pitching wedge is a safer club, but even then you may have too much bounce for such a delicate shot. If that's the case, try the 9-iron.

DEVELOPING DISTANCE

Toots Shor, the late legendary New York saloonkeeper, once said that golf was a crazy game because "to hit the ball hard you have to swing soft." Toots was right, but when golfers try for those extra yards, they do what comes naturally—which, of course, causes all kinds of problems, like tensing up, jerking the club back, throwing the club from the top of the swing, coming out of the knee flex, and spinning the left knee toward the target.

Normally, I try to swing at about 80 percent speed, because that's the amount of force I can fully control. When I need extra distance, I have two swing keys. First, I concentrate on swinging the club away in

a comfortable rhythm and on a line directly back from the ball until I feel it set into what I call the "slot" at the top of my backswing. There's no pause at the top, but if I can feel the sensation of setting the club at the top I know I've made a backswing that is under control and that I've given myself plenty of time to make a good body turn.

I don't rush the downswing, but at impact I like to feel that my right knee and right shoulder are driving toward the ball along with the clubhead as I swing through the ball.

The key words are *through the ball*. The good player swings through the ball, while the weekend player *hits at it*.

SKIPPING A BALL ACROSS WATER

I've talked a lot about playing the odds in this book. Well, here's a shot where the odds are against you, but the situation may dictate that you must gamble. I saw Lon Hinkle hit this shot on his way to winning the 1979 World Series of Golf.

Skipping a ball across water is a lot like skipping a flat stone on a pond. You need to make both the ball and the stone meet the water at the shallowest possible angle. Just think how you drop your throwing shoulder when you try to skip a stone with a sidearm delivery.

To hit this shot, use a 4- or 5-iron, set the ball back in your stance, and set your weight left with your hands ahead of the ball. Make a compact backswing, striking the ball with a sufficiently descending blow to be sure you hit the ball before the ground. Putting a hook or right-to-left spin on the ball will give it added momentum and possibly an extra skip or two, so through impact turn the toe of the clubhead over as you would to hit a quick, low hook.

Before you hit the shot, take a good look at the landing area on the other side of the water. If it's a steep bank without much grass, the risk may not be worth the attempt, because the ball may just roll back into the hazard.

THE "SUPERPITCH"

You're about 125 yards from the hole, looking at an uphill shot into a strong headwind. You could hit a full shot with a lofted club, but there's no telling what the wind would do to the ball.

Here's a safer shot. Take a 6- or 7-iron, open your stance, and set your hands ahead of the ball, which should be positioned inside your left heel. This isn't a shot that calls for a full backswing. Depending on the distance, you might use a half or three-quarter swing. Just make sure you don't rush, which is the temptation any time you shorten your swing.

As the name suggests, this shot is played like the pitch shots we covered earlier. You should pinch down on the ball, making clean, crisp contact with a firmly descending blow. Your hands should be ahead of the clubhead at impact, and there isn't much of a follow-through, just as there isn't on pitch shots around the green.

PART VI

PRACTICE

SOME THOUGHTS ON PRACTICE

It isn't enough simply to stand on the tee and beat practice balls. To practice correctly you must have a goal for every shot. Create an on-course situation in your mind, visualize the shot you have to hit, then hit it. Not only does this help instill the discipline of fully thinking through each shot before you hit, but it forces you to take your time between practice shots.

How often have you heard players complain that, after spending hours on the practice tee, their problems are worse than when they began? It's not surprising, since too much practicing at a time can lead to both mental and physical fatigue, making the practice counterproductive.

I suggest that, once you've established exactly what you want to work on—and remember, you can realistically work on only one or maybe two problems in one session—you quit after achieving your goal. Too often, golfers ingrain one swing fault while spending hours on the practice tee trying to eliminate another.

When warming up before a round, make the last shot you hit on the practice tee the same as the first shot you have to hit on the course. If the opening hole calls for a slight fade off the tee with a 3-wood, that should be the last shot you hit on the practice tee—and make it a good one so that the only thoughts you bring to the first tee are positive ones.

Good players must always fight against hooking or pulling the ball, and that means practicing with a wind coming over your back, quartering from left to right, is largely a waste of time because such a wind negates the effects of a hook or pull swing. The best wind for a good player is from twelve o'clock (head on) to two o'clock (quartering from right to left). These winds will exaggerate the effects of a pull or hook, and will also allow you to practice holding the ball against the wind with a fade—which is a fine shot to have in your bag.

Occasionally, you'll hear a player say that a hole gives him trouble because it "just doesn't look right." That's because that player's normal shot doesn't fit the hole's design, and as a result, he never feels comfortable over the shot.

The same holds true for practicing. I remember going to the Masters and studying Ben Hogan and Sam Snead on the practice tee. Ben liked to fade the ball, so he would have his caddie stand in an opening behind a row of trees that opened up from left to right. He would fade his shots around the trees and land them at his caddie's feet.

Sam was just the opposite. He liked to draw the ball, so his caddie would be tucked off behind some trees down the left side. To hit his target—the caddie—Sam would draw the ball around the trees.

The lesson is, "Never practice against your eye."

THE BASICS OF GOOD BALANCE

I would say that 99 percent of the weekend players I see have a problem with balance. This stems from either trying to hit the ball too hard, or from having a poor address position. Either way, it's a serious problem because it is impossible to develop a consistent, repetitive golf swing if you are forever out of balance.

Here's a good drill to help develop better balance. Get two boards, an inch or so thick and the width of your shoes. Stand on them, assuming your normal address position, with a ball placed on a tee. Now, with a 5-iron, try to hit the ball without falling off the boards.

This will be difficult for you at first, but the more you practice, the easier it will be to stay in balance—and I think you'll be pleasantly surprised at how quickly you begin making better contact both on and off the boards.

THE DIVIDER CLUB

If I had a short time to practice and only one club to practice with, I'd want that club to be a 5-iron. That's because it's what I call the divider club, between the long irons, which are distance clubs, and the short irons, which are for accuracy. The 5-iron is also good because it is equally easy to fade and draw the ball with it, as well as hit the ball lower or higher.

KNOW YOUR DISTANCES

Today, most courses have markers that tell you the distances you face for shots into the green. But what good are the markers if you don't know how far you hit each club?

When I was playing my best golf, I hit my 7-iron 145 yards under ideal conditions. The rest of the clubs varied 11 yards from there. For example, I'd hit a good, comfortable 8-iron 134 yards, a 6-iron 156 yards.

Here's the best way to find how far you hit each club. First, determine just how long a stride you must make to step off a yard. That may sound simple, but strides vary greatly and that can make a big difference when multiplied by, say, 150 times.

Once you've found your stride, take a dozen *new* balls and number them 1 through 12. Go to the practice range and hit all 12 balls, making note of any that are mis-hit, and pacing off the distance to the majority of balls. Then move on to another club until you've worked your way through the entire set.

You'll be surprised by how many strokes you'll save from knowing just how far you *really* hit each club.

THE FOUR-TEE DRILL

Three- and four-foot putts are among the most nerve-wracking shots in golf. The only way to become comfortable with them is to practice them. Here's a drill that will help you do so productively.

Take four tees, setting one on either side of the hole and two more a putter blade's width apart back where you plan to putt from. The idea is simply to roll the ball through the tees. Don't think about the hole, just concentrate on making your best stroke and letting the ball roll cleanly through the tees.

You'll be surprised what a good confidence builder this is, and the reason is, of course, that it allows you to forget about the hole while concentrating on your stroke.

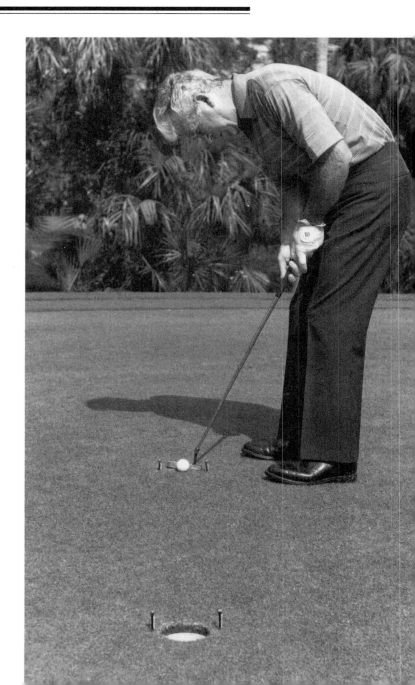

A TIP ON LONG PUTTS

Whenever you have a long approach putt, you should always be thinking distance before direction. A good way to practice these putts is to imagine a three-foot circle around the hole and then concentrate on getting the ball into that circle. Don't worry about the hole or your stroke. Instead, concentrate on the speed of the green, the length of the putt, and the amount of break. If the ball goes in, so much the better, but what you are aiming at is avoiding three-putt greens.

Another good way to develop a feel for distance is to forget the hole entirely and putt balls at the fringe of the putting green. This drill will help you focus on distance rather than direction by eliminating the instinct always to go for the hole.

ONE LAST THOUGHT

The amount you are willing to work on every aspect of your game will largely determine just how much of your potential you will realize.

Ben Hogan said it best when he said that "for every day you miss playing or practicing, it takes one day longer to be good."

If that's true for Ben Hogan, it's certainly true for the rest of us.

KEN VENTURI won 14 tournaments on the PGA Tour between 1957 and 1967, including the 1964 U.S. Open Championship. That same year he was named the PGA's Player of the Year. Forced into retirement from the Tour at age thirty-three by a hand ailment, he has since achieved equal eminence as the golf analyst for CBS Sports, which he joined in 1968. He is highly regarded as a teacher and is one of the few professionals whom Tour players seek out for help with their games.

Born and raised in San Francisco, Venturi is presently vice-president and director of the Eagle Creek Country Club in Naples, Florida.

DON WADE is an associate editor at *Golf Digest* magazine. His writing has also appeared in a wide variety of other publications, including the *New York Times,* the *Boston Globe*, the *Washington Star, Tennis* magazine, *Travel and Leisure,* and *Connecticut* magazine. In addition, he has appeared as a feature reporter for CBS and NBC Sports.